WEB WISDOM

Make the Most of Tumblr and Other Blogging Platforms

Cathleen Small

Cavendish Square
New York

For Theo, who I'm certain will someday parlay his love of elevators and rock music into some strange (and hopefully profitable) career. If anyone can do it, you can!

Published in 2015 by Cavendish Square Publishing, LLC
243 5th Avenue, Suite 136, New York, NY 10016

Website: cavendishsq.com

This publication represents the opinions and views of the author based on his or her personal experience, knowledge, and research. The information in this book serves as a general guide only. The author and publisher have used their best efforts in preparing this book and disclaim liability rising directly or indirectly from the use and application of this book.

CPSIA Compliance Information: Batch #WW15CSQ

All websites were available and accurate when this book was sent to press.

Library of Congress Cataloging-in-Publication Data

Small, Cathleen.
Make the most of Tumblr and other blogging platforms / Cathleen Small.
pages cm. — (Web wisdom)
Includes bibliographical references and index.
ISBN 978-1-50260-195-7 (hardcover) ISBN 978-1-50260-194-0 (ebook)
1. Blogs. 2. Tumblr (Electronic resource) I. Title.

TK5105.8884.S63 2015
006.7'52—dc23

2014017121

Editorial Director: David McNamara
Editor: Andrew Coddington
Senior Copy Editor: Wendy A. Reynolds
Art Director: Jeffrey Talbot
Designer: Douglas Brooks
Senior Production Manager: Jennifer Ryder-Talbot
Production Editor: Sam Cochrane
Photo Research by J8 Media

Printed in the United States of America

Contents

CHAPTER 1

Blogging: The Major Players

You've heard about people blogging, and maybe you even follow a few blogs regularly. Now you've decided you want to write a blog of your own. You've got something to share and people to share it with. It's time for you to get out there, jump into the blogging waters, and share your message with the masses! Just one question remains, how do you start?

In the world of blogging, Tumblr, Blogger, and WordPress are the three biggest sites, so they're the ones we'll talk about. You will find that these three blogging **platforms** provide you with more than enough options to build a creative, interesting blog that people will want to follow.

You're probably itching to get started and share your ideas with the world. Before you do, let's talk a little more about these three major players in the blogging world, so you can decide which one is best for you.

Microblogging with Tumblr

The **microblog** Tumblr is a somewhat new platform, having been launched in 2007, but it's a major entity, **web hosting** more than 180 million blogs. In June 2013, Tumblr became part of Yahoo! in a $1.1 billion deal. That's not too shabby a profit for a little platform created by its founder during a two-week break between tech contracts! Currently, more than 101 million Tumblr posts are created each day. That's a lot of blogging!

Why Is Tumblr Right for You?

Let me start with a very simple question: Are you at least thirteen years old? If not, then Tumblr isn't the platform for you. You must be at least thirteen years old to use Tumblr, no exceptions. Think I'm kidding? Check out their terms of service, or the rules which one must agree to follow in order to use a website, on the Tumblr website and you'll see.

Now, assuming you're at least thirteen years old, you should know that Tumblr is very popular among young bloggers—particularly teenagers and college students. In fact, at least half of Tumblr visitors are under the age of twenty-five. Part of the attraction may be that Tumblr is a microblogging site, which is ideal for young people who are busy with school, homework, sports, and other afterschool activities. If you have something to share, but not a lot of time to share it, then a microblog might be the perfect platform for you.

You may be wondering what a microblog is. If you break down the word, it's exactly what it sounds like. "Micro" typically means "very small," and "blog"…well, you know what a blog is, or you wouldn't be reading this book! A microblog, therefore, is a very small blog. Posts are usually short—maybe a few sentences, or perhaps just an image or video link. If you want to discuss heavy, complex thoughts on deep topics, then a microblog probably isn't your best platform. However, if you want to share a quick thought, a video you just shot, or even a couple of images, then a microblog is an excellent place to do so.

Blogger: Simple and Straightforward

Okay, what if you're not yet thirteen years old, but you still want to blog? Or maybe you are thirteen already, but you're interested in a true blogging platform, as opposed to the microblogging features offered by Tumblr. What's the best option for you?

Well, one option is Blogger. It's simple, tried-and-true, and will let you do almost anything you want when it comes to creating a blog, be it writing text, posting pictures, or uploading videos. Best of all, you can do it at any age! The only catch is that if you're under the age of thirteen, your parent or guardian must set up your account for you.

Blogger has been around for a long time. Launched in 1999, it was one of the first blog publishing sites available. Its simple, straightforward interface, or computer system, allows even blogging newbies to quickly and easily set up an appealing site.

Blogger became even more user-friendly after being acquired by Google in 2003. Google quickly integrated Picasa, its image-sharing platform, into Blogger, making it easier than ever for Blogger users to post image galleries. In 2010, a Blogger redesign gave users access to many more blog **templates**, or formats, making blogs more customizable.

If you're not yet thirteen years old, you'll need to have a parent set up a Blogger or WordPress account for you.

Why Is Blogger Right for You?

If you're interested in having a flexible blog that is relatively easy to create, then Blogger is an excellent choice. Blogger lets you write as long (or as short) a post as you want, and adding pictures or videos is a snap. It is also great for groups of people who contribute to the same site. If you want to create a collective blog where people other than yourself can post, Blogger supports that feature.

WordPress: The Big Daddy of 'Em All

Not sure whether Tumblr or Blogger quite fit your needs? Maybe it's time to think about WordPress. Almost a fifth of the top 10 million websites were created with WordPress, and currently there are more than 60 million WordPress-created websites out there. As with Blogger, if you're under age thirteen, you just need your parent or guardian to set up your WordPress site for you.

As for how long it's been available, WordPress falls smack in the middle of Blogger and Tumblr. It was created in 2003. It quickly grew in popularity as users recognized its flexibility for creating almost any kind of website you can think of.

Think WordPress might be too much for you? After all, you're just starting a little blog, and major organizations use WordPress to host massive websites! Think again. WordPress may be a giant in the field, but it's actually very simple to use and perfect for hosting a blog. In fact, I use both WordPress and Blogger for my own blogs, and I am definitely not a major corporate empire!

Why Is WordPress Right for You?

If you're not interested in a microblog, then the best place to start is Blogger or WordPress. Both are good choices, but if you're interested in more flexibility for your blog design, then WordPress is where you want to be. It's slightly more challenging to use than Blogger, but that doesn't mean it's difficult.

WordPress is so popular that many, many people have developed **widgets** that you can use with your WordPress site. For example, I wanted to add my Instagram **feed** so that it could run along one side of my blog. My simple WordPress template didn't have that feature, but I quickly found a widget that would let me do just that! These little ways to customize your site are what sets WordPress apart from Blogger in terms of blog creation.

Now that you've learned about some of the options for creating a blog, it's time to get started!

NETIQUETTE

One thing you will have to remember while blogging is to practice **netiquette**. When you post something online, people reading or viewing it can't see your body language or hear the tone of your voice. What you might think is a joke could end up offending someone who doesn't realize you meant it as such.

So, how can you observe proper netiquette? Follow these simple guidelines:

- *Never post when you're angry.* If you feel very heated about something, don't hit the Post button until you've had a chance to walk away from it and calm down.

- *Never, ever bully.* Cyberbullying is very real, and unfortunately it's becoming quite common. You never know who you might hurt and how badly. Take the high road and keep any unkind thoughts to yourself. A blog is not the place for them.

- *Give credit where credit is due.* Never pass someone else's work off as your own.

- *Be clear and calm in your posting.* Write simply and clearly, with proper grammar and spelling. Avoid using all capital letters or a lot of boldface type, which can sometimes seem as if you're yelling at your audience.

- *Always, always stay safe.* That's the number-one rule on the Internet: Be safe. Keeping yourself safe from online predators is crucial. Never share personal details about yourself online. Be wary of anyone who befriends you online and then suggests you meet in the real world.

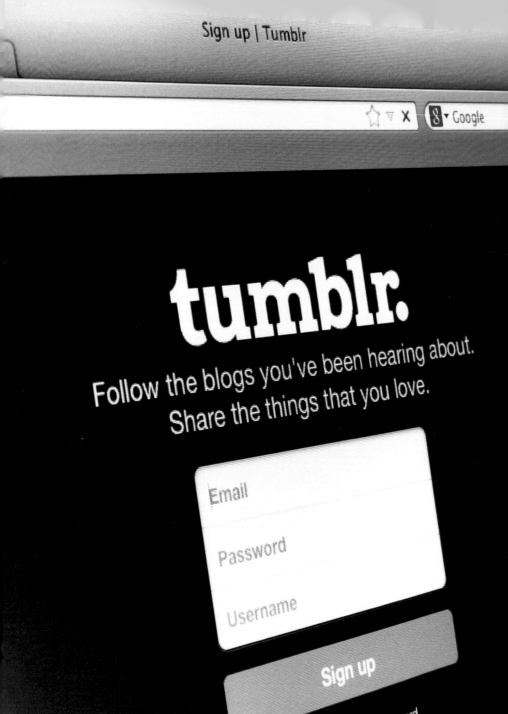

CHAPTER 2

Let's Get Blogging!

All right, it's the moment of truth! Time to launch that blog you've been thinking of. Are you ready? Grab a bottle of water and a snack, sit down at your computer, and summon up all those creative ideas brewing in your brain. You're about to blog!

Text-Friendly Blogging with Blogger

Let's say you want to create a traditional blog where you can write posts and maybe insert some pictures and videos. We're going to start with Blogger, which balances text creation with media sharing.

Create Your Blog

Blogger is a Google platform, so you need a Google account of some sort to create a blog. For example, many people have their own personal or school Gmail account for email. If you do, then you're all set. If not, it's easy to create a new Gmail account. Just go to *gmail.com* and follow the instructions.

Once you've logged into your Google services, you can create a new blog. Go to *blogger.com*. You'll be greeted with this screen. You'll see that you can create a Google+ profile, but for now let's use the easy method, the Blogger profile. Click on "Create a Limited Blogger Profile." You'll be asked to choose a display name, as shown in the following screen.

Once you create a name, you'll be taken to a screen with a "New Blog" button in the upper-left corner. Click that button.

Now you can title your blog, choose a **URL**, and pick a blog template. Do so, and then click "Create Blog!"

Creating a blog on Blogger is as simple as entering a bit of text and clicking your mouse.

YOUR BLOGGER PROFILE

When you look at your published blog, you might notice the "About Me" section on the screen. The default location for this section is on the right of the screen, but depending on the blog template you choose it may be somewhere else. Your default profile is pretty generic, but you can spice it up by clicking "View My Complete Profile" and then clicking "Edit Profile." Just be careful what information you include. Remember that anyone can view your blog and profile. Including details about where you live or where you go to school is not wise. Keep it general. It's fun to have fans of your blog, but it's important to keep yourself safe from strangers who may be following your blog.

That's it, you're now a blogger! However, you're a blogger with an empty site, so let's keep going.

Write Your First Post

After you click Create Blog!, you'll be taken to the Blogger dashboard. This is the same screen you'll see each time you log in to Blogger. Click the orange pencil icon in the upper-right corner to write a blog post.

You'll see that the "Create Post" page is quite simple. In fact, the interface looks a lot like Microsoft Word and other word processing software. Below the post title and above the field

You can create your first blog post in a matter of minutes.

for the body of your post, you have a toolbar that allows you to change the font, size, and style of your text; add web links, images, and videos; and even create bulleted and numbered lists.

Type a post title in the "Post" field at the top, and type the text for your post in the big box below the toolbar. Play around with the toolbar buttons to format your text. Go ahead, you won't break anything!

When you're finished with your post, you can click the orange "Publish" button in the upper-right corner. Or you can click "Save" or "Preview," next to the Publish button, if you want to save your post for later or preview what it will look like when published to your blog.

Writing posts is not the only thing you can do on Blogger. You can also add multimedia, such as videos and photos. These can spice up your content, making your blog more entertaining and visually appealing. However, if you really want to do the most with your media, Tumblr, the next site we'll discuss, does it best.

Say It with Pictures in Tumblr

The microblogging site Tumblr is best suited for short posts, images, and videos. Think of it kind of like an advanced Twitter: It's short and sweet, but you can do more with it than you can with Twitter.

Create an Account

The first step is to head over to *tumblr.com*. You'll see that the account creation screen is pretty simple. All you need is an email address, a password, and a username.

You'll be asked your age, and you'll need to check that you've read and understand Tumblr's Terms of Service. When you have done that, click "Done!"

A confirmation email will be sent to your email address, and you'll need to click on the link in it to verify your email address. Then you can log in to Tumblr, where you'll be greeted by the Dashboard.

If you want to take a tour of some of Tumblr's features, you can click on the "Show Me Cool Stuff" button in the middle of the screen. Otherwise, you can just figure it out on your own, which is a great way to learn the site and its features.

Add Media

Adding images, videos, and even audio clips is incredibly easy in Tumblr. To add a photo, click on the "Photo" link at the top of the page. You'll be taken to an upload screen where you can upload up to ten photos. Just click on the little camera icon in the middle of the screen to get started. When you've finished choosing images, you can enter a caption. Then, when you're finished, click "Post."

To add a video, click on the "Video" link at the top of the screen. You'll be taken to a screen where you have two choices. You can either embed code or a video URL, or you can choose a video file from your computer. Choosing a file from your computer works much the same as choosing an image file to upload, so let's talk about how to use the video URL option instead. If you are using a video from YouTube, you can visit the site and copy the URL, then paste it into the field on tumblr.com. A preview will load, and you can add a caption before you click "Post."

You'll probably spend more time snapping the perfect selfie than you will posting it to Tumblr—it's that easy to do!

Is there a particular song you're loving right now? Click the "Audio" link to add it to your Tumblr blog. You'll be presented with a box where you can search for a song, upload one from your hard drive, or use an external URL link to a song.

The "Search" field is a cool feature. You simply type in the name of the song you want to add, and Tumblr will search for options for you. You can then click on the version you want to add, add a description of the track, and click "Post."

Tumblr has a mobile app to make updating your microblog even easier.

GIVE CREDIT WHERE CREDIT IS DUE

It is easy and smart to **copyright** content such as pictures that you share on your blog. I include a copyright on all of my photos to keep others from being able to use them without my permission. I don't mind sharing, but I want to make sure no one takes and alters my images without my consent.

The truth is, whatever you create is valuable to you, and you'd undoubtedly like to receive credit for it if someone else wants to use it. Similarly, you should extend that courtesy to others, too. Millions of people create interesting content and are willing to share it. Some will even allow you to alter it to suit your needs. If you choose to use someone else's work, make sure to give them credit for it. Protect your own work, too, so you don't end up in the unfortunate situation of having your work used without your consent. Believe me, it happens, and it sometimes isn't pretty.

There's an easy to way to protect your work, and it's called Creative Commons. A Creative Commons **license** is essentially a free, simple copyright license that gives you a standardized way to grant permission for others to share and use your work under your conditions. Maybe you're willing to share your content with individuals, but you don't want it used for commercial purposes. You can specify that through a Creative Commons license. Creative Commons licenses are highly customizable, so you can choose whatever terms best suit your needs.

Please note that Creative Commons licenses don't replace copyright; they work alongside it. If you want to learn more about Creative Commons, visit *creativecommons.org*.

CHAPTER 3

Using WordPress Like a Pro

Maybe you have moved past the basics of blogging and are yearning for more. Maybe you'd like to be able to do more than just post text, pictures, and video. Perhaps you want to integrate widgets on your blog, or truly customize your design. If so, then WordPress is the answer.

Create an Account

As usual, the first thing you need to do is set up an account. Go to wordpress.com and click on the "Get Started" button.

On the sign-up page, you'll be prompted to enter your email address, a username, a password, and your desired blog address.

Click "Create Blog" at the bottom of the page when you've entered the information and WordPress has verified that the blog address you want is available. On the next page, you'll get a chance to customize your site title and add a **tagline**.

WordPress may be a major player in the web-design world, but setting up your WordPress blog couldn't be simpler.

Choose a Theme

Once you've created an account, it's time to choose a theme. Some theme templates are available for a fee, but many are free. Take your time and scroll through the options to find one that perfectly reflects the style you want for your blog. If you click on a theme, you'll see a page that tells you the features of the template you've chosen. If you like what you see, click "Customize It!"

I like to write, so I've chosen the Writr template for my blog, which is a simple template well suited to short written pieces. If you're more of a graphics person, find a template that places images at the forefront.

You'll see that WordPress set up my blog with a very simple version of the Writr template. On the right side of the screen are options for "Color," "Header," "Site Title," and "Theme Options." I can click on any of those to customize my design. You should see similar customization options with any template you choose, but they may be in a different location on the screen. Just poke around and look for them.

After you've finished customizing, WordPress will take you back to its setup **wizard** and ask you if you want to connect your blog with your Facebook or Twitter account. This is a great idea if you're looking to publicize your blog a bit!

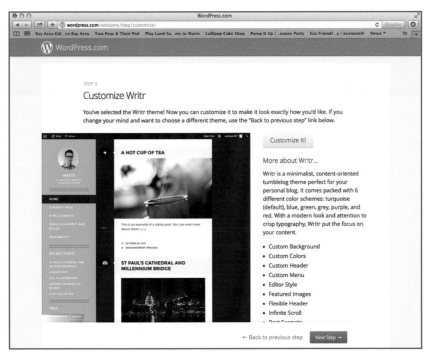

You can customize WordPress's included templates.

Publish a Simple Post

Can you believe we're ready to publish already? The WordPress wizard allows you to create your first post out of text, a photo, a video, a quote, or a link.

For our purposes, let's start with a photo post. The wizard tells you exactly what you need to do. If you can successfully create a post on Tumblr or Blogger, you'll find WordPress to be just as simple.

Customize Your Site

Okay, so how do you take this further than a simple post? Do you see the words "Blogging from Cali" at the top-left of my site, next to the WordPress logo? Look closely, it's just a small link. Look for a similar link on your site, and hover your mouse

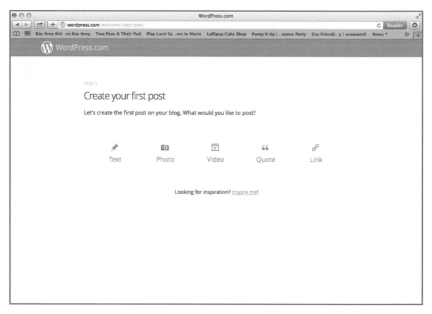

WordPress gives you simple, clickable options for creating your first post.

pointer over it. A list of options will pop up. Click on "Dashboard."

There are so many options to explore in the WordPress dashboard! If you're feeling overwhelmed, you might want to visit their "Zero-to-Hero Guide" for a quick tutorial. Look for the link in the middle of the dashboard, to the left of the "Welcome to WordPress" video.

The left side of the dashboard is full of clickable options. You can view your site **stats** if you want to know how many people are visiting your blog and how they're getting there. You can track the comments you've made and the blogs you follow.

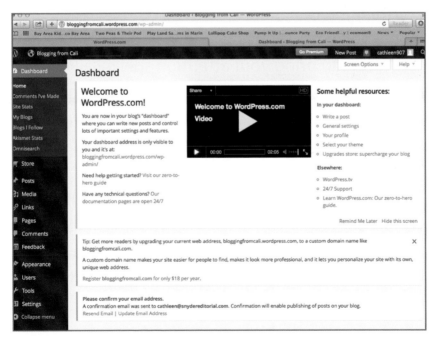

The WordPress dashboard is your go-to place to do virtually anything with your blog.

You can create new posts and pages, reorganize your current posts and pages, track and manage incoming comments, and create polls to get feedback on your site. Just click around on the links on the left side of the dashboard to see all that you can do.

WordPress is very user-friendly in terms of explaining their features and what you can do with them. If you don't understand something, hop on Google and search for it. WordPress is so widely used that for pretty much any question you have about it, you'll find a quick answer on Google. WordPress bloggers are quick to share their knowledge of the platform, which can be a huge help when you're starting a new blog.

I want to bring your attention specifically to the "Appearance" link in the dashboard. Click on it, and you'll see that the option expands to give you access to "Themes," "Customize," "Widgets," "Menus," "Background," "Custom Design," and "Mobile."

This is a part of WordPress that you'll probably visit frequently. If you're like me, you might like to change up your blog theme regularly, just to keep things interesting. This is where you'll go to do it. No need to go through the wizard again—you can just do it from your dashboard.

If you don't necessarily want to change the

entire theme but you want to spruce it up a bit, try clicking on the "Customize" or "Background" item under the "Appearance" link to play around with your site's look and feel.

If you have a little spare cash, you can even click on "Custom Design" to access advanced site design options. You'll have to pay for the upgrade option, though so make sure it's worth it and you can afford it.

You may want to customize the menus that appear on your blog. Just click on the "Menus" item under the "Appearance" link to reach a page where you can design your menu hierarchy. This

The "Menus" item in WordPress will let you customize the menus that appear on your blog.

can be useful if you want your site to be more than just a blog. Perhaps you want to include pages on your interests, links to other blogs you enjoy, recommended reading, or any number of other things. Menus can be your best friend for organizing this type of content.

Add Widgets

Widgets are one of the things that makes WordPress so cool. A widget is essentially a fun little tool that you can add to your site. There are tons of widgets

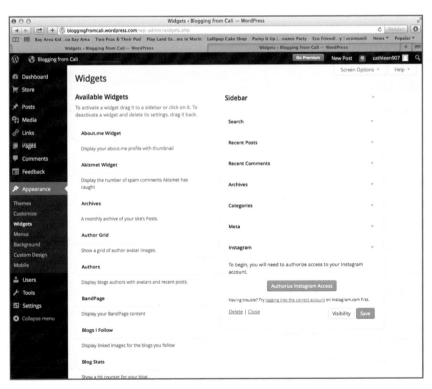

Widgets may be the most fun part of WordPress. You can go widget-crazy on your blog if you want to!

available for *WordPress.com*, and even more if you eventually upgrade to *WordPress.org*.

Do you want to display a hit counter for your blog, so people can see how many visitors you've had? There's a widget for that. Are you interested in adding calendar of your posts? There's a widget for that, too. How about including a Facebook "Like" box, so your blog readers can connect to your Facebook page? There's a widget for that. There are widgets to add a "Follow" button so people can easily follow your blog, for displaying your latest Instagram or Flickr photos, a music player, and your Twitter timeline. They're all there, and many more.

The configuration for each widget will be different, but they all share one thing in common: ease of use. *WordPress.com* is designed to be extremely user-friendly, and it will generally walk you through anything you want to do on your site.

There's a lot more I could tell you about the WordPress settings and how you can track your site comments and stats, but the best way to learn WordPress, or almost any blogging platform, is to just start playing with it. Take your time. You'll be amazed to discover how much more there is to blogging with WordPress, and how easy it really is.

CHAPTER 4

Case Studies

You now know how to build a blog using Tumblr, Blogger, or WordPress. You might even have created your site and your first post by now. However, one simple post does not a blog make! Let's explore what some bloggers have done to take their blogs to the next level.

Pizza with Sam

Sam is fourteen years old. He loves playing baseball and Minecraft. He also loves pizza. In fact, Sam loves pizza so much that he has tried every pizza restaurant in his hometown. He has decided to share his pizza knowledge with the greater public, and a blog seems like a perfect way to do just that.

Sam decides he wants to start with a simple blog. He's not into fancy designs. He just wants a site where he can post his reviews of pizza restaurants with a few pictures for each. He knows his reviews will be a couple of paragraphs long, so he decides to use

Blogger instead of Tumblr. He likes microblogging on Tumblr for the personal blog that he shares with his school friends, but for his pizza review site, he wants something a little more comprehensive.

Sam decides to name his blog Pizza in Parkside, since he lives in a neighborhood called Parkside and most of his reviews will be for restaurants located there. He quickly builds a simple site through Blogger. Sam wisely keeps his profile information very vague. Readers of the blog will likely know he lives in or near Parkside, because that's where he reviews restaurants, but that's all he wants them to know. After he creates his site, he edits his user profile carefully. For his profile picture, he uses an image of a delicious-looking pizza slice. He chooses not to specify his gender or his location. All he wants his readers to know is that he's someone who likes pizza served in the Parkside area.

Sam's friend has clued him in to the fact that he may be able to earn a little money on his blog, so he goes to the "Earnings" tab on his Blogger dashboard and enables Google AdSense. He doesn't mind a few ads on his blog if it'll bring in a little cash. From there, he can choose whether he wants to receive payment in the form of a check, electronic transfer to a bank account, and so on.

Sam is also active on social media, so he makes

sure to post on Facebook and Google+ every time he writes a new pizza restaurant review. His site gains followers, and before long he has a pretty decent audience.

Sam can now start contacting pizza places in his area that he plans to review. Some of them, particularly the smaller, non-chain pizza joints, are so excited about the publicity that they offer Sam a free meal in exchange for his review. That doesn't mean that Sam necessarily has to write a positive review, by the way—the pizza restaurants know that he plans to review their food honestly, and they just hope that their meal is tasty enough to earn them a great rating from pizza-master Sam!

The Newest Generation of Bloggers

There are many kids who have become successful bloggers. Blogs come and go, and some kids start blogs and eventually abandon them to pursue other interests. However, there are some young bloggers who have stuck with it and become quite successful.

Alex, the Sunday Diner

Alex is a kid from Connecticut who loves going out to breakfast with his dad. Together, they created a WordPress blog called Sunday Diners: A Kid's Guide To The Best Diners And Breakfast Spots In Fairfield County, CT… And Beyond! (sundaydiners.com), and it has become quite popular. Alex and his dad, James, publicize their blog on Facebook and Twitter, and they've been profiled in *Food Network* magazine, *Good Housekeeping* magazine, and in several regional newspapers and websites. Colorful and eye-catching, Alex's basic website design is also simple. It has just four main pages: the homepage containing the blog posts, an About page where readers can post a message to Alex and his dad, a page with links to all of their favorite diners, and a page that lists all of the publications and press in which the blog has been featured. Alex also tags each blog post by town. This organizes them into a clickable menu along the right side of his homepage. Readers can click on a town listed in this menu and immediately link to all the blogs Alex has written about restaurants there.

Baseball with Matt

Matt is a fifteen-year-old from New Jersey who loves baseball. His current favorite team is the Yankees. He loves the history of baseball, too. Matt decided it would be fun to share his knowledge of baseball with other kids and adults who have a similar interest in the game, so he started a Blogger blog. He is, in fact, the youngest professional baseball history blogger currently on the Internet. Matt's blog is so popular that he has been featured on

MLB.com (the official Major League Baseball site). His success should serve Matt well, since his career aspirations are to be a baseball broadcaster, journalist, or historian!

Matt's blog is called Baseball with Matt: A baseball history blog for kids (and adults too) ... written by a kid blogger (*baseballwithmatt.blogspot.com*). He posts new blog entries several times a week, which he then publicizes on Twitter, where his handle is @BaseballwMatt. The site design is extremely simple, just one page. Along the right side of the page you'll find a baseball history news feed, links to press and publicity about Matt's blog, and fun links to interviews Matt has done with baseball greats Hank Aaron, Yogi Berra, Curt Schilling, and even former president George W. Bush! How did a teenage boy from New Jersey manage to interview such huge names? It's simple. Matt has built quite a name for himself as a knowledgeable, passionate, and dedicated baseball blogger, all with a simple Blogger site.

Emily Jane

Emily Jane is a fifteen-year-old blogger from Australia who dreams of becoming a fashion designer or somehow working in the fashion industry. Emily is no stranger to blogging. At the age of ten, she created a blog called CraftyGirl,

Emily Jane took her love of fashion and made it into a blog. She now receives more than 25,000 page views per month on her popular blog.

where she posted about her love of crafts. As her passion for fashion grew, however, she decided to start a new blog called, simply, Emily Jane (*emilyjane.typepad.com*). Since its debut in 2013, she has expanded it to include everything from fashion to photography to everyday life, all from her unique perspective. Emily Jane has gained an impressive following, averaging more than 25,000 page views per month. That means about thirty-five people visit her blog every hour!

Emily Jane's blog is so popular that it has been featured in numerous fashion magazines and websites. She has also taken it very seriously as a business opportunity, and actively encourages advertising and industry collaboration on her site. She sells ad space for a nominal fee, collecting the payments through a PayPal account. She also encourages retailers to send her clothing that she incorporates into fashion posts to promote their business. In addition, her blog is **sponsored** by a dozen different brands.

Emily Jane is a Typepad site. Typepad is a flexible blogging platform that allows extensive customization as WordPress does, but there's one catch: You have to pay for a monthly subscription to Typepad. The price isn't particularly high, with plans currently starting at $8.95 per month, but you can design a similarly impressive site using WordPress, for free!

Feeling inspired by these blogs? Go on out and create, design, and promote your own blog. With blogging, your opportunity is as limitless as your creativity!

GLOSSARY

copyright The legal right that protects works of literature, drama, music, and art.

feed A summary of frequently updated web content.

license A permit that allows you to own or use something, such as a piece of writing or art.

microblog A blog designed for short, frequent posts, rather than more extensive posts.

netiquette A polite, respectful, acceptable way of communicating on the Internet.

platform Software used to create a blog.

sponsor An entity that supports or funds a given project or activity.

stats Short for statistics. Stats describe data about your site, such as the number of page views, the number of unique visitors to your site, the hours that your site receives the most traffic, and so on.

tagline A slogan or catchphrase. Many bloggers use a tagline in addition to a blog title to identify their blog.

template A preset format for a document or web-page. In blogging, you can use templates so that each page of your blog has a consistent look and feel without having to recreate it each time.

URL Stands for Uniform Resource Locator. A URL is a web address.

web host A company that provides space on its server for webpages. If you want to use your own web host, you generally have to pay to have your site hosted.

widget A small gadget. In the web world, a widget is a little piece of software that can run on a webpage.

wizard In computer-speak, a software feature that automates complicated tasks by walking the user through a series of questions.

FIND OUT MORE

The following books and websites will take you on the next step in your blogging journey.

Books:

Gunelius, Susan. *Blogging All-in-One for Dummies*. 2nd ed. Hoboken, NJ: Wiley, 2012.

Gunelius, Susan. *Google Blogger for Dummies*. Hoboken, NJ: Wiley, 2009.

Jenkins, Sue. *Tumblr for Dummies*. Hoboken, NJ: Wiley, 2012.

Sabin-Wilson, Lisa. *WordPress for Dummies*. 6th ed. Hoboken, NJ: Wiley, 2014.

Websites:

"The Beginner's Guide to Tumbr"
mashable.com/2012/06/03/the-beginners-guide-to-tumblr
This article from Mashable.com provides a step-by-step guide to opening and using a Tumblr account.

"How to Blog: A Step-by-Step Guide"
amylynnandrews.com/how-to-blog
Writer Amy Lynn Andrews' website for bloggers includes tips, tricks, links, and more.

"How to Use Blogger for Beginners"
susancarter.hubpages.com/hub/How-To-Use-Use-Blogger-For-Beginners
This HubPages.com article by ebook writer Susan Carter includes insider tricks for setting up your blog on Gmail's Blogger platform.

"Seven Ways to Make Money from Blogging"
www.mint.com/blog/how-to/7-ways-to-make-money-from-blogging-0513
Kelly Anderson provides basic information about using AdSense, ebooks, and more as a way to earn money by blogging in this MintLife.com article.

"WordPress How-To for Beginners"
www.siteground.com/tutorials/wordpress
This tutorial on SiteGround.com includes the answers to the most frequently asked questions from WordPress users.

BIBLIOGRAPHY

"About." Tumblr.com. http://www.tumblr.com/about.

"David Karp and Tumblr." YouTube video, posted May 27, 2008. https://www.youtube.com/watch?v=D-K4pLXWkgMw.

Davis, Sammy. "So What Do You Do, David Karp, Founder of Tumblr?" Mediabistro.com, August 27, 2008. http://www.mediabistro.com/So-What-Do-You-Do-David-Karp-Founder-of-Tumblr-a10281.html.

Farber, Dan. "Tumblr for iOS Launching Next Week." CNET.com, June 15, 2012. http://www.cnet.com/news/tumblr-for-ios-launching-next-week/.

Gunelius, Susan. "How to Make Money from Your Blog." Dummies.com. http://www.dummies.com/how-to/content/how-to-make-money-from-your-blog.html.

Liedtke, Michael. "Yahoo Takes Big Leap with $1.1B Deal for Tumblr." 6abc.com, May 20, 2013. http://abclocal.go.com/wpvi/story?section=news/national_world&id=9105444.

"New and Improved Blogger Mobile Apps." Buzz.Blogger.com, November 15, 2012. http://buzz.blogger.com/2012/11/new-and-improved-blogger-mobile-apps.html.

"Press Information." Tumblr.com. http://www.tumblr.com/press.

"Terms of Service." Tumblr.com. http://www.tumblr.com/policy/en/terms-of-service.

"The Story of Blogger." Blogger.com. https://www.blogger.com/about.

"Usage of content management systems for websites." W3 Techs: Web Technology Surveys. http://w3techs.com/technologies/overview/content_management/all.

ABOUT THE AUTHOR

Cathleen Small is an editor, teacher, and author who lives in the greater San Francisco Bay Area. She has been blogging on various platforms for several years about her travels, the adventures of her two young sons, and her fearless pugs. You can find her at *foursmalls.com* and at *smallpeanuts.blogspot.com*. When she's not busy raising her boys, working, or blogging, Cathleen is always on the lookout for the next great adventure and the next tasty slice of pizza.